FORGIVING
JUDAS

Macabre Ink is an imprint of Crossroad Press Publishing

Copyright © 2015 Tom Piccirilli
Cover illustration by David Dodd
Interior design by Aaron Rosenberg
ISBN 978-1-941408-20-9 — ISBN 978-1-941408-21-6 (pbk.)
For information address Crossroad Press at 141 Brayden Dr., Hertford, NC 27944
www.crossroadpress.com

First edition

FORGIVING JUDAS

POEMS

TOM PICCIRILLI

DEDICATION

If you've already missed your last chance, if your future is all behind you, if your ghosts keep you awake at night whimpering, if you still can't shake a lost love no matter how hard you've tried, if your scars are faint but still visible, if you can reach inside your own gut and withdraw shards of knives you placed there yourself, if you can't fight any harder than you already do, if someone has to remind you to forgive yourself, if you still have work to do, this book is for you—

And to T.M. Wright—

And to Ginny—

And of course to the living poetry of my life, Michelle—

CONTENTS

PART I

Running naked
down the icy avenues
of night

FORGIVING JUDAS

I am Lazarus sliding the stone aside,
groping in darkness, mute, choking on the black
Without even the squeaking of rats or bats
to guide me back to the world,
God's light fails, God's voice is an immutable breath,
I await the angry angel Azreal to commit me
to the pit, as I sit and patiently await for Lucifer to visit.
I have lost all dreams,
all fantasies, all memories
And given them to the dust,
except for when I write and come alive.
At thirteen I awoke in the morning angry and mean
And stayed that way for twenty years.
Would I have thought so much of suicide if I only knew how hard
I would one day fight for my life?
I remain stolid and solid only because I am stuffed
Full of regrets, fears, cancer, love, and sins.
If only my mother could forgive me for my aimless transgressions,
My ingratitude. My betrayals. My lack of a kind word. My inability
to speak my heart and thankfulness.
Outside the rock are sacrifices left behind. Oil and lamb and dried
    fruits
I eat in the moonlight. I wash with the oil and dream to burn
It's the only yearning
The finality of my learning.
There is so much drama, theater, posturing, and screaming.
You all need to just calm the fuck down
Like all those nice cool, quiet people in the ground.

THE SEA, LOVE, AND PERDITION

She was hot, beautiful, sensual, sweet, and she liked me
So I blew it, of course. A head full of bad wiring, neuroses,
    commitment and intimacy issues
Balled up on the floor beneath her like a dirty tissue. She tried and
    tried to care
But I was beyond all that. I cried and cried to tell her beware
But she didn't believe me, licking my hand, finger by finger, as we
    drove to
The sea, she didn't believe me
Until, with pained, hateful, injured, disbelieving eyes,
she finally did.
We live and die by small crushes. Our favorite new songs, new movies,
New actresses, new heartbeats, new posters for our bedroom walls,
    it's always
Been this way. I am twirling my little blue flashlight, I am doing
    what I do
I am looking up. At my father who always sits so close, with one
    muscular arm around my shoulders
up, up, up at the trapeze flyers, at the wire-walkers,
At the big kids seated higher behind us in the bleachers.
The world terrifies me because I do not understand
I will never understand.
You are surrounded by the living and the dead, but
You are alone. There's no helping it. You live inside your brain, inside
    your skull, you
Own what you own because it was hard-won. You will die there too.
When it happens you will hold out your hands, you'll reach for mama
For daddy, moaning, for anyone. You'll claw to hold on as you slip
    inch by inch
Over the rim and down the Cliffside
Of perdition.

4

RUNNING NAKED DOWN THE ICY AVENUES OF NIGHT

Like many of us, I am inchoate
Unfinished, searching for a way to complete myself.
To refurbish, to find recompense, to revise the draft.
What else is there to talk about?
What else is there to do?
There must be something. I traipse through my head
Looking for a time of adventure, action, heartbreak,
and instead
I just find emotion, raw sewage-like emotion. This is why I write
stories, so I can fill in the broad blank spots of living and stuff them
With activity of one sort or another, which I never did really do,
Never did perform, never did attempt, never did attack, never did
    vanquish,
Never found in the deserts or the mountains, the ocean, the edges
    of rivers, the
back yards of childhood, the cold streets of blackness. I live in the
    whiteness
of the empty page
Because it is cleaner there than in my embittered brain, my false
    histories
My missed opportunities, my weak dream-quests. They say you
    regret the things
you didn't do
not the things that you did. I regret
both.
There must be something to this, running naked down the icy
    avenues of night
Otherwise, all the best maniacs wouldn't be doing it
In front of my house all the time.

I HAVE LIVED MANY LIVES

And then the dreams come with tidal force
Where I awaken without knowing where I am,
Who I am,
Who my wife is, or remember how to breathe.
And I live somewhere else,
And my wife is someone else,
And I am someone else.
I sweat in fear, in acknowledgement of madness,
The taste of seaweed kisses in my mouth,
In the throes of darkness on my belly.
I have lived many lives at night.
The alternate dimensions of possibilities confront
Each other between midnight and dawn. Perhaps I'm
A boxer, or a chef, or a cop, or a billionaire philanthropist
With a carload of kids. We're off to a picnic, a school play,
The choir, a soccer game, sometimes I'm dead, sometimes
I'm somebody named Ted, or Al, or Bill, or Fred. And when Fred
Goes to bed, he sometimes sees me, peering at him from inside
his head.

IN THE GLOOM

We sat in back
In back of the movie theaters
In back of the restaurants
In back of the bars
In back of our cars,
Wherever it was dark, so we could make out
So we could fondle each other beneath the tables
Whenever we were able. It ended badly, it always
Ended badly. It had to because of me. We drank our
Drinks and stared in opposite directions. When she took up
With my best friend I understood. I drove by her house
In the gloom, and soon he was there with her, and soon
They were together in a new house, and I drove by there at the
Haunted three am. And his other girl. His last girl, his lost girl,
was parked across
The street, watching the well-lit windows with vulture eyes,
Terrified as if she had died. I told
Her to leave. When she finally did, I pulled into the space, and took up
Her cause, which was also mine. It hurt but not quite enough to drive
me away back home.

WE RE PRACTICALLY
THE SAME GUY

We're practically the same guy
Rarely is he mentioned without my name
Following, or his mine. Reviewers, fans, editors,
They say we share themes, images, styles, voices.
They say he's unique. They say I'm unique.
Because we share in the poetry and pain of life, because
We have our regrets. He battles illness and weakness,
he goes in and out
Of the hospital, as do I. He's got heart issues, I've got
brain issues. I watch movies with sad music and I need
Lots of tissues. Somehow he beat the odds, somehow I'm
Still here.
He's got daddy issues, mommy issues, me too.
He often feels blue, I can often be blue.
He married a writer, I married a writer. He looks in the mirror
And sees me looming. I look at my reflection counting my scalp
Scars. Forty-seven staples, but there seems to be more
scars than that. He shares his work with me, and I with him. It's
been that way pretty much since the start. He is art. I am art.
Glad to meet you, art, we're
Art.

GRAND CANYON BURNING

After twenty-five years she got to within a few minutes of me, a
    couple miles away, as if that were
always her true intent,
Her real purpose, searching me out like a storm of memory, a
    blizzard of youthful revelations,
a lightning flash of mournful kisses.
What could I possibly want from her now? All these years later,
    with both of us firmly set
In our lives, why would I still get any kind of a rush seeing photos
    of her at the Grand Canyon
With her husband and kids? But the ego is still there, I still want her
    to notice me, it's chemical,
It's conditioned, it's no
different than ninth grade science class. Me, the school fool, talking
    out of turn, making bad
Jokes, whatever I could do to get on her radar, and failing even that,
    mostly. But we are driven
Forward by the old nerve endings, the old welling of need, of want
    and connection, her smile
Still makes me blaze
like the canyon on nuclear fire.

BRENTWOOD LIBRARY CIRCA 79

Why am I stamped the way I am? Why
Do I recall what I recall, why imagine these things
And run them out into storylines that sink back
Into my depths. Is it all regret or guilt? Is it all
Fabrication? Elucidation? Manipulation? Is it all
About what's been lost? Is it all jealousy because
I'm still an ungrateful brat who can't be glad for what
I have? Am I just hammering on the church doors, trying to
Turn back time? I am still alive in the library, still waiting for her,
And her mother to drive me home,
in Nineteen seventy-
nine.

JAPANESE CANCER LIE

It's time for the oaths of apologies again
Ma's been gone twelve years already, and I
Never really knew how much I loved her until I couldn't
See or speak to her anymore.
Joe, my step-father, doing his best with me, as ignorant
As I was educated, always arguing facts. This morning he
Is claiming that three atomic bombs were dropped on Japan,
Says the third one fell on Tokyo, says he knows this because he was
There and felt the ground heave and rumble. Me, getting out
    encyclopedias
Trying to prove my point, but such things are unprovable to such
    people.
Flustering him so much that he needed an extra shot and beer that
    morning, my Ma
Upset with me, ordering me to apologize. Me, dragging feet to the
    kitchen table,
Saying I was sorry. Joe, saying it was okay, always saying I had book
    smarts but no
Common sense. He spoke the truth, at least there he did. Him,
    down with cancer
Shortly thereafter, a trache in his throat so he couldn't talk anymore,
and who the hell cared how many atom bombs fell in the Pacific
That day, or any day, while he died, and my mother cried,
and I lied.

TIME TRAVEL TANTRUM

We lose our legends, and we lose our heroes, they all leave us
    eventually
Like our fathers and girlfriends. We miss them and the missing
    grows every day, every year
As we feed them more and more of our energy and dreams and
    willpower. Because we
Want, we want them to continue, we want to hear their voices again,
    we want them not to be
Dead and done. We want things to be the way they were, and like a
    child turning blue
Holding his breath on the edge of a tantrum, I will sit here until I
    have everything I've lost.
I am a time traveler
I set the machine for Italy 1943 and I'm running with Patton,
Doing my duty, hard, a hero on the road, storming the Germans,
A perfect shot, a perfect brother in the band,
Then I'm home again on the GI Bill, putting my house together,
Married with sons, grandkids, asking me what I did in the war.
And now it's the late 60s and I'm not quite a hippie, a Vietnam vet
This time, who knows what he's talking about when he talks of war.
Hair, Marine-cut short, but with long sideburns, riding a chopper,
    on the road,
I'm balanced, a counter-culture hero, someone who visits the
    communes,
Gets laid by the hippie chicks but doesn't take advantage, a teacher,
    a guy
You don't mess with. If the redneck townies come around to kick
    ass, I show the
The right way to do it. I go to bars and see fellow vets down on their
    luck, about
To throw tantrums of their own, holding steak knives, grabbing up
    forks, and

I move to them, disarm them without fuss, offer my help, get them
    to the psychs

At the VA. I step in and out of my machine and go everywhere and
    anywhere, always

Me, always a hero, muscles bulging, fighting, a protector, always
    doing what

I do best in my stories.

I'm back in the time of Christ, staring up at the cross, his blood
    dripping on my hands

And I ask, "Do I stop this? Tell me to stop this, please." He knows
    my secret, he knows I wear

Two thousand years of dust. I ask again, and he shakes his beaten
    head, the crown

Shakes down more droplets of sweat and blood, and I sink to my
    knees.

QUALITY OF WRITING

You want to know the time? Why do you want to know the time?
   I'll tell you
The time.
Anyway, it's 1:23 pm, on a Friday. March 14, 2014. Now you know
   what I know.
I'm waiting for Michelle to awaken (she's a night owl and sleeps
   late) so we can go
To the rec center and swim for a couple hours. My balance is still
   pretty weak, I tend
To wobble and drift, to stray to the left, to weave around like a
   drunk,
swimming helps restore
My balance, helps to keep me on the straight and narrow. But I still
   can't drive, so I
Wait for my devoted wife, my life, my sweetness, so we can swim
   in the lazy river pool
That tugs us along and swings us wide around the corners. So here's
   something I was
Thinking about, when my sweet niece mentioned that she read my
   book in one long sitting,
Couldn't put it down until she finished it at three a.m., and her
   father, my brother, sensing
That might've shined my ego or ass a little, made sure I was
   grounded again, and told me,
That has more to do with her lifestyle, staying up really late, than
   with the quality of your
Writing.
Consider me grounded. Consider me no longer full of myself after a
   compliment. Consider me,
But not for long. For I am now
Dashed, mashed, crashed, bashed, hashed, and slashed.
There he is, ladies and gents, my brother,

with his arms red up to the elbows in my blood, from plying around
In my guts.
Defender of the realm,
Guardian of the family.

PILGRIM NIGHTS

Suffolk County Community College shared land with Pilgrim State
    Psych Hospital. They sat

Across a small road from each other, teachers' cottages beneath
    cherry blossom trees facing

Hundreds of rows of cube windows with ten thousand empty eyes
    and hollow faces refracted in them.

We would

Go to class all day and then grab our girls and a few six packs and
    drive the perimeter of Pilgrim

In our trucks to where huge holes had

Been clipped in the chain fencing. It was dark as the devil's eyes
    back there on the manicured lawns

of the mad, slug-like moon sticky above crawling across black
    construction paper sky

the wind strong enough to kill.

The ping pong palaces of the maniacal and depressed, the nymphs,
    the catatonics, the chronic

masturbators, in there they sometimes sing, or chant, or scream, or
    weep loudly enough that all the

nearby houses turn on their lights.

I imagined parents making a wrong turn off

the highway, heading left instead of right, and driving by the
    enormous housing facilities of

The hospital, asking anyone they saw on the walking paths,

"Mrs. Hansen's office? Mrs. Hansen? English Literature?" while
    nuts in

Stolen sweaters and lab coats responded, "Oh yeah, please bear to
    the left, Mrs. Hansen will be

With you shortly."

And we would drive up and down the back roads of night, imagining
    ourselves behind the glass cubes

In a year or two, twenty-one or twenty-two at the oldest,

depressed, stressed, wrecked, drunk, addled, hurt, pissed, pressing
    noses against windows,
Hissing, "Mrs. Hansen? Mrs. Hansen? My homework is
Done."

PART II

I might be
a noir hero
suffocating on despair

DOC SAVAGE SUNLIGHT OVERLOAD

So who am I today? Not myself, never myself
Maybe I'm a long haul trucker who battles witches,
Maybe a reporter trying to track down a pulp writer who knows
Where Atlantis lies. Maybe a poet without any poetry left, with
Only memories of rhymes, but no reason, in mid-season, waiting
For spring to arrive. The dishwasher groans and swirls, the dogs next
Door bark and yowl, my dogs howl, my wife rolls east, and I watch
    from
Another room, brightly lit with sunlight
for the first time in weeks, I might be a super-hero, I might be
my father, I might be a private eye breaking an investigation, I might be
a noir hero suffocating on despair, waiting to kill, waiting to die,
I could be Doc Savage, the Shadow, the Spider, or the Phantom, Tarzan,
More innocent heroes, some claim, though not me, they're as dark as
The rest of them, maybe even darker, maybe even worse, in their
    way. It's
Only right I should be them today with the sun baking the world,
    and the dogs
Barking out my brain.

MINOR CELEBRITY

I'm not exactly a medical marvel but at least I'm not pushing up daisies
Yet. A year and a half ago they told me I had a 2% of making it a year.
2% motherfuckers.
So my oncologist, neurosurgeon, and radiation specialist want to write
Some articles about me and my progress, and what it's like to be
    alive when so many others
With this type of brain cancer are dead. What's it like? Feels much
    better than being chowed on
By worms, I can say that much. I didn't really do much besides keep
On breathing and not lay down. I owe my life to the docs, my wife,
    my friends, my family,
And the fans for all their generous words, cards, emails, letters, etc.
The hospital's going to send their marketing
People around to do a piece on me since I'm a "minor celebrity."
Well, hell, better that than being
A major one planted underground.

BOBBY, AT THE END

I think about my step-brother, Bobby, more than ten years dead
Never learning from anything, two busted marriages, caterwauling
   women,
five kids who hated him,
Never holding on to a good job, driving a taxi, driving a bus, getting laid
In the back, the seventeen year old Puerto Rican girls keeping him
   hoping,
The twice-divorced women with adult acne and forty pound beer bellies,
Told to stay there in their seats and wait for him, who sit on the bus,
   waiting,
Digging his dick enough to degrade themselves that much, while
he runs into the house to grab a shot of scotch, maybe some lunch,
   his father and
My mother peering out the window, looking at the bus.
"Who's that? Is someone still on there?"
And he answers, "Just a friend."
Handsome in an old Elvis kind of way, one shirt button too many
   undone,
Thick Sicilian mustache, perfectly groomed fifty minute coif hiding
   the bald spot,
stealing all he could from whomever he could, owing his uncles,
   begging cash,
both of them pissed, calling him a scumbag liar,
watching his father die,
watching my mother die, watching himself die in ignorance,
weaken, sicken, changing color, turning yellow, hepatitis A or B or C,
an alphabet of disease,
on the couch, watching TV,
shitting blood, finally wanting to die.
Saying he wanted to go home, he wanted to go home, please, Tommy,
Tommy, Tommy, Tommy,
let him go home,

23

and me, with my voice cracking along the cold, stone floor of obvious
    truth, having
to say it because he still didn't know, couldn't know, wouldn't know,
having to frame the words and tell him, "Bobby,
Bobby, Bobby, Bobby,
you have no home."

TWO OF MY HEROES MITCHUM AND WILLEFORD

Nothing to do at four a.m. but stare out the broken bedroom window,
listening to the freight whistle pipe as the train crawls across the cold
blue moon plains. It's the loneliest sound in the universe this side of
a woman crying, as the slow chug of the boxcars dwindles down the
tracks to the south. I think about guys like Mitchum who was forced
    out
of his home during the depression, too many mouths to feed, so at
    fourteen
Mitch rode out there alone, a real man, a real young man, a star in
    the making,
His strides already giant upon the Earth.
I think of guys like Willeford, who did the same, a hobo at ten
    looking for a bowl
Of stew, fluent in bindle-speak. Hopping trains, seated in the camps
    as the war
roared its way towards him. He ran his own tank crew, got racked
    up with shrapnel,
I wonder what it would have been like if they'd run into each other
    at the same soup kitchen
Would they have been brothers on the road, or would they have
    squared off, the two toughest
Kids in the west.

TWO TICKS AFTER I LEAVE

Two ticks after I leave, I'll be back
For a final walk-through. Count on me catching you
With my kidneys in your pocket, my pencil stubs
In your pen-holder.
After the last witch is burned,
And the last worm has turned,
And the last lesson learned,
After the last fool has danced,
And your eyes have failed, and your hand has failed,
The rats will still scamper in the corners and the dogs
Will cry alone in the dark,
and the cat will mewl and scratch, and
two ticks after I leave, the doctor will still want samples
of my stool, and the lab
Will hand you plastic and gauze and tube and wire,
And the door will swing wide in welcome and affront,
The storm will punch in and out, the world will ask
If I have learned anything about life, death, the turning of the clock,
about man, about God, Satan, goldfish, kindness, hope, and
I'll tell them, "I learned everything I needed to know, somehow, jester
and loser that
I was, including how to
strut down the middle of Main Street in hell."
Then I'll fall down, and then I'll get up, and then it'll be me
And Pete staring at each other at the gates, his wizened face
Not so wise as mine.

I MISS MY FRIENDS

I miss my friends
who chose their angry, flat-faced snarling wives over me
The nights we smoked out cigars and watched bad action movies
And drank some beer and
the world didn't turn on my cancer or their lack of courage or
their wives' fat asses.
It's almost summer again and I stare up and down the empty street
Searching for them, I suppose, and wonder if they're actually, truly
Happy in those dark halls and on living room couches
being hissed at
Shouted at, berated, not so silently hated,
Climbing into beds at night as sour
As rotting lemon groves.

LIGHT LINES

Slept way late, awoke to them arguing downstairs about rock 'n' roll,
The history of dead guitar stars, each of them trying out the voice,
Discussing prices for the signatures, the smashed instruments,
The clothes, the posters, this guy twenty years dead, all magazine
Articles talking about the death of rock, the rebirth of rock, the
  maiming of rock,
I think about it. Maybe they're right, maybe not. I'm still half-asleep,
  can't
Really add anything except these lines, as a listener, as an observer,
  I let them
Continue with their enthusiasm even though they're so loud, so
  energized, I
Rarely have such passion anymore, and
Now the dogs are being inspired to sing too. Up on their back legs,
  dancing,
Nails clicking, but we're in the midst of more drama,
late last night at the bar where they work,
The manager went nuts wanting part of their tips, the manager
  lucky to be a woman,
Or they would have kicked her ass. The drama overflowing into
  today, into tomorrow,
Her lying about the bar, leaving it dirty, money the issue, everyone
  wanting to quit.
The manager, drunkenly cooking and claiming she's as good as
  them. The drama, the theater
Persists, far outweighing the depth or heaviness of these light lines.
  My wife emerges into
The office, and now the conversation changes, she's talking about a
  cop that got shot in town
A few weeks ago, how they never caught the culprit, some kid out
  joyriding, so why would he have
Had a loaded shotgun in the car, and why would he use it? I posit

that men are more afraid of
Prison and rape than death, thanks to the TV shows, the graphic
    movies of dicks in asses, of
Lying on your knees, being set on fire in cages.
Despite my occasional fantasies of walking off with bundles of cash
    from banks, I would
Never try it thanks to Oz, Prison Break, Sons of Anarchy, Cool Hand
    Luke, The Longest Yard,
shows of such sadism, and
Yet, as I know, not as sadistic as life,
as the spittle truth.

ANOTHER FUNERAL

At another funeral but I can't remember whose. I crane my neck for
    a look
At the coffin on the altar, but it's closed-casket. I try to spot faces,
    grieving wives,
Mothers, anyone to recognize, but I can't see. The priest reads a few
    passages,
No help there. Which friend, which lover, which family member?
    Great-aunt
Olympia? Linda? Harlan? Gerard? Terry? Who's old and dead,
and who's young and finally
Sucked the tailpipe, chewed the rat poison, edged a razor into the wrist,
Stepped in front of the train, put the bullet into the ear.
Who got caught in an earthquake, who lost it to cancer or congestive
Heart failure? The priest is onto Psalms, could be anyone, sit, kneel,
    rise,
Sit, kneel, rise, sit, kneel, rise, bow, smell the incense. Linda liked
    incense, burning it
In the bedroom, little spark of red in the dark. I lean left, I lean right,
My wife looks at me askew and asks, "What are you doing?"
I would tell her but she might be offended, it might be her best
    friend, her sister, her
cousin, her Aunt Kathy, another priest, the pope,
nope, can't say, can't admit I don't remember shit.
I wait for the priest to finish
up and finally get to revelation.

A WALK ON THE BEACH

It's not easy not remembering,
I get flashes that are like the tentacles of
A great sea beast yanking me beneath the waves,
tidal force tears me off the
Beach until I'm a thousand fathoms deep. The pressure is so great
  that my
heart is in my throat, my ribs are snapped like anchovy spines. It's
  so silent that
The voices, images, kisses, slaps, and laughter drives me even
  deeper, drowning
And thankful for it.
I want silence in the shipwrecks, I want silence in the mouth of the
  serpent,
I want silence at the desk, in the chain, on the lawn, in bed, but my
  head
Is full of nothing but the roars of memory,
tsunamis, sirens, and screaming sailors.

GOODBYE, TERRY

Goodbye Terry,
goodbye those poetic masterpieces of madness, murder, death, life,
    psychic
powers.
And ghostly resurrection, goodbye to those strange seeds, those
    eyes of carp,
Those blue canoes, those stone soups.
Goodbye Terry, although you're not quite gone yet,
but according to your wife your mind has flown its coop.
Sometimes mine does the same. Take wing and ride the wind.
At least so far as I know, you're
In no pain, you no longer know the difference between
sane and insane.
Goodbye, TM, you deserved far better in life
and in this non-life, but I'll still call
You friend until the last minute, whichever last minute is your last
    minute, and
Whichever last minute is
Mine.

HOT CHICK FULL OF HATRED

I'm not so angry anymore, most of the time, but when the rage hits,
it takes savage bites from my throat, my soul, and my head,
I have a trench across the top of my skull where the neurosurgeon
Went in and dug out the cancer.
Under the thin skin and thinning hair
are three or four metal plates that look like steel snowflakes. Pretty
  little bitches,
my scalp is scarred from staples,
not stitches. One of them probably
pinning down a zen nerve, spewing calming endorphins,
The rage moves along my spine, makes me glare into the horizon with hate,
I don't even have to know what I'm pissed at now. There's a wealth to
  choose from,
names and faces, mostly gone or dead,
or so changed they don't even matter much anymore.
Yesterday we walked into the pool and some hot chick was sitting on
  the sidelines. I turned
my heard and smiled, and she glared with such open ferocity I
  wondered what the fuck I
Possibly could have done to her or her kids, who were swimming
  wildly in the short end.
And yet when the rage hits I have to place it at the feet of someone or
  something
besides me. So maybe she's got to do the same thing. Her hurt, vicious
  eyes spiking me
to the nearest wall. As I hit the water, I sink and think of her up there
  reviling me
for imagined slights. I turn it around and think of her butchering my
  heart, taking me apart,
inch by inch, until in the locker room her husband hunts me down
and tears out my sexy plates
one by one with his teeth and spits them into the shallow end,
just like my own awful ugly sorrow and confused revulsion.

33

WRITER'S CONVENTION

The days of hopping into my car and splitting across the country to
    meet a woman
at a convention, steal her from her husband even as she is stolen
    from me, moving
out of my room and into his. He had more power in the biz, a big-
    time editor, looked
like a fucking ferret to me. He was married too, two cheaters doing
    their thing,
me young and
naïve as a Down's syndrome baby. Standing in my hotel room with
    a scotch in hand,
The liquor fanning the flames, the burn making me turn mean,
staring out the window of a strange city, listening to
The hallway. The giggles, the drunken caterwauls, folks fucking in
    the room next door,
security guards rushing this way
And that, parties on other floors getting too loud.
Me, shy, lonely, mostly unpublished, without money, without real
    skill, a nobody, a nothing,
With no career to speak of, no big editors in my pocket, no famous
    writers singing my
Praises, nothing to offer the woman who always needs to be offered
    something,
except my love, myself, imagining him on top of her, making
    promises of bestsellerdom, inviting her out
To dinners with celebrities and stars.
My trouble back then was I didn't understand that you
Actually find what you're looking for. I didn't want intimacy so I
    didn't get it,
If you want a hot whore who cheats and looks over your shoulder
For the next one coming up behind you, you'll get her.
That night he sent her to the train platform, promising riches and

34

    fame and greater love,
and then he went back to his wife,
and she went back to her husband,
and I went back to my car and the road, drove home,
and got down to business.

PART III

I should've played dead
She would have respected me
More

TAXES

Tax time again. I fucking hate it, gathering up receipts, going
   through the credit cards,
Writing off whatever I can, checking my credit score, making sure
   everything is in place,
Nearly had a heart attack doing this a few years ago, blood pressure
   landed me in the hospital, 200
Over 100. Nurse looked surprised I was still alive, stared at me like
   I had to be the walking dead,
shocked I was still breathing, but
The lady from billing wasn't that wide-eyed, with her hand out
   while the docs stuck nitro patches and
IVs in my arms and chest.
"How are you going to pay for this?" she demanded. My pants were
   on the floor, I should've played
dead, she would've respected me
More. Now it's here again. Last year we filed late because I was so
   out of it on chemo,
only a few months have gone by, and we still had to pay late fees
   and interest.
I want to see my name on a school, or on a fixed pothole, or someplace
   to show the money got through.
They're doing work up the road, maybe
a placard, or a plaque, something commemorating my cash, my
   efforts, the late fees, I want a street
sign with my name on it. DETOUR FOR TOM. PIC CROSSING.
   SLOW FOR PIC. PIC AVENUE. The
construction guys all waving me through like I'm the champ, the
   prez, an astronaut returned to Earth, a
foreign king.
Numbers, I hate numbers, I'm right-brained, still need my fingers to
   count, so I decide to clear my head.
I turn on the TV and put on a martial arts flick

Starring one of the world's most beautiful women. The film fuels
    the fantasy. I'm quicker than Bruce,
Stronger, my story is hipper, cooler, I'm not laid out like cold deli
    meats, and the woman is impressed
with my muscles, my skill, my speed, and she comes Into my arms
    between my enemies,
and I hold her and kiss her brow, speaking Chinese, and for now
That's all I need.

I Tried to Drown Her, But She Wouldn't Sink

Swimming at the rec center pool tonight, kids splashing and thrashing like crazy,
Reminded me of when I was about eight and went to the town pool, accidentally
Kicked a girl my age and apologized, but she glared dead-eyed as a shark and got out
Ran to the lifeguard and pointed at me. Guy motioned for me to come see him, so I did, but
The lifeguards had this particularly sadistic little game they played with kids they didn't like,
Punishing them for things like accidentally kicking little girls.
One would whisper some nonsensical
phrase and tell you to run to the other end of the pool
and relate it to the other lifeguard down there.
And then that one would send you back again. "Go tell her that Grandma doesn't like syrup on her
Meatballs."
And then you'd run back again.
"Tell him that Cicero enjoys the sites of Venice."
Until you were out of breath and wanted that smug little shit of a girl dead in the water.
Today we watched the baby swim class, babies bobbing in their lifejackets, and I was reminded of
something else too, how when I was only
two or three my mother took me into the tub and let me slide down her knee, and she explained to me
that before I was born she had had another baby in her belly
but that baby had died.
For years, in my head I imagined that kid hadn't been torn out,
flushed out, but had stuck around, whispering to me
through the water all the secrets
of the never-quite-born.

41

JESUS PEOPLE AT MY DOOR

The Jesus people came around again today,
and invited me to save my soul
by reading their pamphlets.
The literature wasn't about love or kindness or friendship,
But about THE BIBLE. Do what THE BIBLE says or suffer eternal
  agony.
Come to the church
And learn all about it under the tutelage of some old fart
with white Abraham hair and a perfect part,
Come early and you will get a free gift!
(A FREE POCKET BIBLE)
I almost mention that all gifts, by definition,
are free.
But I don't want them to whip one out, hurl it into my face,
and break my nose.
They have that kind of
look, like if I said no they might burn my house down
to show me the error of my ways, glaring
at me like I was a centurion.
Of course, it's in Matthew 10:34 where Christ says, "Think not
that I am come to send peace on
Earth: I came not to send peace, but a sword." Again, I come this close
to saying something,
But I just can't handle the look of sadness
and anger in those bitter brown Christian pudding eyes
anymore.

A DAY IN COLLEGE

She was stupid with sex and stupid with lies, and her laugh
Was laced with near-hysteria, eat-shattering and making everyone
Turn in their seats to look. Across the hall the Dean lounged in his
   doorway
checking us all out.
There were about eight of us in class who were after her, and she
   made damn
sure she didn't make eye contact with any of us. Didn't smile directly
   at us.
In the halls of higher learning we all got dumber
and dumber watching her. Chuck moved his seat to her left, Richie
   went right,
Don closed in from behind, and like the perfect pupil I sat ahead of her
facing the board, feeling her breath on the back
of my neck. The professor called us up one by one to read our poems
   and stories.
Sal had something about her flaming red hair and nearly broke into
   tears,
Fred read a piece about loving someone until
dead, Jasper couldn't hold a candle to any of us and knew it,
and tried to plagiarize Ernie.
He got caught two sentences in, Prof went nuts and gave him an
   instant F.
The rest of us glowered, she laughed again and Jas threw his
   notebook
out the window. She was in a green dress that day, tight, curvaceous,
wild hair, wild lipstick, wild hint
of a wild thong peeking out of her hip-hugging jeans
and Joe went with something from out of his journal, honest, full of
   real names,
pointing at the class as he hit line after line like a Gene Krupa set,
his voice growing stronger and

stronger, Prof impressed, the rest of us too, and we started tapping
    our desks in time
with his rhyme,
and soon we stomped our heels,
and soon we all knew the words
and we were all singing and swinging
together, a band of morons at her mercy.

THE DAY MY BROTHER WROTE ABOUT THE DAY OUR FATHER DIED

So where am I now? Back in Hicksville, upstairs in the room I shared
   with my brother, my room
Given to Grandma, who came to stay after Dad died. Mom worked
   nights, my brother too,
So me and Grandma would play Italian card games and listen to
   the Mets, and watch TV....
Kung Fu, the Waltons, Little House, Friday Night Movie of the Week.
My mother didn't let me attend the funeral,
thought I was too young
And that it would scar me.
Instead the scars came from not attending, not sharing my grief
   with my loved ones.
My brother kept a journal, and I went through it,
but only that day, Nov. 4, 1972,
where he wrote what the day was like for him, started
off, "It pissed rain today." With a little drawing of rain falling on a
   headstone.
I read the page over and over and over,
and then one day the journal was gone.
He'd kept it "hidden" at the bottom of the drawer with other shit on
   top of it,
not much of a hiding spot really, and I had placed it back wrong so
   he knew I'd looked.
He said it was a violation, an Invasion of privacy, what I did, reading
   his private thoughts.
But I was seven and the ass didn't understand that I didn't give a
   damn about his fucks,
his troubles, his time in local jail

45

cells for robbing houses with his friends, playing tag in Macy's, his
   beliefs on the nature of the Vietnam
War. No, I just needed to be there when they dropped my father in
   the dirt,
in the rain. I had grief that couldn't come to conclusion
And still hasn't.

OLD DREAMS

Heading back to the beach in a couple of weeks,
if only there were enough money that we could move to it
for good, and live there for the lasting. When will Hollywood call,
When will the big one hit, when will the Nigerians send me my
hundred mill.
They keep promising and I keep hoping.
I had a dream last night about an actress I had a crush on
when I was about fifteen. We had a picnic on the sand
and she kissed me slowly. My wife must've seen because she spit
on the carpet as I tried to explain.
I awoke with a start. I must have a head full of bad wiring, what
is it that pushes me back and back and back so constantly,
back and back and back to
College, back to high school, back to grade school, back into the arms
Of a forty-year-old fantasy. I lift a hand to my lips and still feel her
   warmth
There. Trust me, it's some spooky shit, dreaming of fifteen and
   waking up
fifty.

A REAL PAIR OF ACES

We don't have Satellite TV anymore, was just too costly, so now we
    make do
With all the movie sites and download sites. I keep thinking about
    when I was a kid
Watching three channels on a fuzzy black and white ten-inch TV with
    rabbit ears,
Sitting there with my grandma trying to make something, anything,
    come through clear
How might she have taken it if I'd told her some day we could load
    thousands of movies in
And watch every old show we ever saw together. Including Italian
    classics. She'd sit in
her rocking chair playing solitaire during commercials, lick her thumb,
    use her thumb to draw
A card, snap the card so loudly it was like a rifle shot. I can picture our
    neighbors wondering, "Who
The hell has a gun in there? Who are they killing?" And me, waving
    them along, "Nothing to see here,
Just my Grandma doing her thing." We were especially fond of Kung
    Fu and the Waltons. When I heard
The opening music to those shows I'd jitter with excitement, and she'd
    say, "Tommy, you love the
Waltons and Kung Fu, don't you?" And it was true, I did, and she did
    too, swinging faster in her rocking
chair until the crocheted blanket across the back of it would flip up
and go sailing across the room. Later on the
house was rearranged so that the big brown box TV was brought into
    Grandma's sitting room
and we could watch that instead, me on the floor stretched out, my
    neck on a pillow,
the pillow against the table, her slippers against my back, and
the cards whapping and whapping at the commercial breaks, me and
    my Grandma quite a couple
back then, a real pair of aces.

INSOMNIAC

Insomnia hits more and more, here it is almost eight a.m. and I still
Haven't been to sleep.
My days are too filled with reading and watching DVDs,
I never really get tired anymore, not like when I helped my buddy
    with his moving
company and would sweat off three pounds in an afternoon. My
    days are filled
With naps, especially during chemo. I need to get outside and rake,
    trim the trees,
fix the lawn up.
Really knock myself out. Funny to be so afraid of the churning
    black sea
but then to want to push
myself down into it again.

PART IV

Tonight's not the night
for the ghosts of dead poets
to giggle in the underbrush

INTERVIEW

Got a call from the hospital's publicity department, who want to
    send out an interviewer
And photographer to do a story on me, since I've (so far) beaten the
    odds. Scary to think
They want to do a piece because it feels like more pressure to stay
    healthy, stay alive,
The docs are counting on me to make them look good, believe it,
    that's part of my reason
For not wanting to fall down. I wonder what her questions will be.
    "Do you believe in God?"
"No, I believe in the love of friends, family, and the positive energy
    of my fans."
"Have you been left in the world for any particular purpose?"
"No more or less, I guess, than the purpose I had before. Do as well
    as I can for as long as I can."
And the photographer snapping pictures like a paparazzi. I know at
    least one set up they'll have
me do. "Hold your book up! Higher! Higher!" I've got fifty pictures
    of me holding my books up
And smiling, looking like a sixth-grader essay winner.
Let me just sit here scowling like a brilliant
Writer, my hands flashing in the air, doing amazing things.

THE WIND

The wind is really ripping it up out there tonight
Like a tribe of rampaging howler monkeys. The branches scratch,
the windows warble,
The chimney wheezes full of dust, the shingles zip to and fro onto
the back lawn,
The leaves skitter, trees limbs clack together like castanets, the car
alarms swing
Into action up and down the street. There are shrieks, screeches,
moans, ominous hisses.
The split-rail fence in the front yard creaks and tilts,
And my wife and I sit with our dogs gathered comfortably on the
bed with my grandmother's
Blankets around us all like her loving arms.
Tonight's not the night for the ghosts of dead poets to giggle in the
underbrush,
But live ones to do their work.

Sad Mom

Michelle is having some trouble with her daughter again.
She hasn't called in months and the last time she did she was pretty
    nasty. Michelle tries
to get her to come around, asks if she wants to go to the movies,
    come to dinner, etc.,
but Melissa just shuts her down.
Now Michelle says Melissa is very mean and makes her feel as bad
    as her mother once did.
I remember a few years back on my birthday when Melissa came
    for a visit
and never wished me a happy birthday.
Instead she mentioned to her brothers, "So what are we going to get
Daddy for his birthday?" Daddy's b-day came about a week after
    mine. Then she'd ask, "And
What about for Father's Day? What should we get *Daddy* for Father's
    Day?" Daddy who had
never done a damn thing for her. In any emergency she'd come to
    me, when she needed someone
To teach her to drive, it was me.
And I'd tell Michelle, "There's no way it's a coincidence, she's got to be
trying to get under my skin."
And my wife would say, "No, she's not
like that, she'd never do that."
But I knew she was and did, and now, sadly,
my wife knows too.

BUDDY

A friend just admitted that he's been depressed for six or seven
    years, ever since
The bottom fell out of the economy and he almost lost his house and
    his life went
Pretty much scorched Earth. I told him about the nearly twenty
    years I was in the blackness,
Drinking and showering with my clothes on, weeping to my mother
    how I needed to
write but just couldn't sell anything. I was out of my mind with
    loneliness.
She had no idea what the hell I was all about and kept
asking, "Why did you do this? Why?"
He says he doesn't believe in therapy or meds,
But I tried to point him that way anyhow.
I know how there's a great deal of guilt that goes
Along with it. You know there are a lot of people much worse off,
    and you feel like
a shit for feeling like shit.

THE BERMUDA DEPTHS

She laughs at me for watching awful 70s horror movies. Burl Ives
   flying a helicopter
Into the head of a gigantic Bermuda turtle and exploding. Ghostly
   Connie Sellecca with glowing white
eyes, Carl Weathers being dragged to the bottom of the ocean.
She says, "What in the hell is this?" I tell her but it makes no
   impression,
not like it made on me when I was twelve.
These are the films that remind me of myself,
the child I was, the sense of wonder despite the stupidity,
we get from a kid's point of view. The jittery excitement I once felt I
   can almost feel
again. A made-for-TV flick from thirty-five years ago that almost
   elicits the same response in my gut.
These are the nutty itches I need to scratch no matter how ridiculous
   or expensive.
"Why do you watch shit like this?" she asks, and I stare down at the
   coffee table
at my morning pills, my evening pills,
the Diabetes pills,
high blood pressure pills,
chemo pills,
all these hills of pills,
And compared to them, Burl Ives and some shitty helicopter
   miniature model fx
crashing into a big turtle
Is a godsend.

NEARLY TIME

Nearly time for another MRI, to tighten up my love handles as they squeeze

Me tightly into that iron lung-like machine. They give me headphones and ask

For what kind of music I like. I say classical or classic rock. It begins to play beneath

The machine's banging and bonging. I sometimes nod off, sometimes I just zone out

Writing in my head, thinking about the next story, the next book, the next poem.

Sometimes my shoulders are wedged so tight against the sides that when they

Pull me out, there's this great roar of air from my lungs. They speak to me over the

headphones. "How you doin' in there, Tom, this next scan will last nine minutes."

"Fine," I tell them. Most guys my age have been in MRI's for their messed up knees, fucked

back in high school, not because of brain tumors,

but I never did think I was much like

the next guy anyway.

ABOUT THE AUTHOR

TOM PICCIRILLI is an American novelist and short story writer. He has sold over 150 stories in the mystery, thriller, horror, erotica, and science fiction fields. Piccirilli is a two-time winner of the International Thriller Writers Award for "Best Paperback Original" (2008, 2010). He is a four-time winner of the Bram Stoker Award. He was also a finalist for the 2009 Edgar Allan Poe Award given by the Mystery Writers of America, a final nominee for the Fantasy Award, and he won the first Bram Stoker Award given in the category of "Best Poetry Collection."

Curious about other Crossroad Press books?
Stop by our site:
http://store.crossroadpress.com
We offer quality writing
in digital, audio, and print formats.

Enter the code FIRSTBOOK
to get 20% off your first order from our store!
Stop by today!

Made in United States
North Haven, CT
20 August 2022

22944336R00043